LAKE CLASSICS

*Great Short Stories
from Around the World I*

Honoré de
BALZAC

Stories retold by Emily Hutchinson
Illustrated by James Balkovek

LAKE EDUCATION
Belmont, California

LAKE CLASSICS

Great American Short Stories I

Washington Irving, Nathaniel Hawthorne, Mark Twain, Bret
Harte, Edgar Allan Poe, Kate Chopin, Willa Cather, Sarah
Orne Jewett, Sherwood Anderson, Charles W. Chesnutt

Great American Short Stories II

Herman Melville, Stephen Crane, Ambrose Bierce, Jack
London, Edith Wharton, Charlotte Perkins Gilman, Frank R.
Stockton, Hamlin Garland, O. Henry, Richard Harding Davis

Great British and Irish Short Stories I

Arthur Conan Doyle, Saki (H. H. Munro), Rudyard Kipling,
Katherine Mansfield, Thomas Hardy, E. M. Forster, Robert
Louis Stevenson, H. G. Wells, John Galsworthy, James Joyce

Great Short Stories from Around the World I

Guy de Maupassant, Anton Chekhov, Leo Tolstoy, Selma
Lagerlöf, Alphonse Daudet, Mori Ogwai, Leopoldo Alas,
Rabindranath Tagore, Fyodor Dostoevsky, Honoré de Balzac

Cover and Text Designer: Diann Abbott

Library of Congress Catalog Number: 94-075349
ISBN 1-56103-048-1
Printed in the United States of America
1 9 8 7 6 5 4 3 2

CONTENTS

Introduction 5

About the Author 7

The Mysterious Mansion 9

The Thing at Ghent 35

A Passion in the Desert 41

Thinking About the Stories 75

❦ Lake Classic Short Stories ❦

"The universe is made of stories, not atoms."
    —Muriel Rukeyser

"The story's about you."
    —Horace

Everyone loves a good story. It is hard to think of a friendlier introduction to classic literature. For one thing, short stories are *short*—quick to get into and easy to finish. Of all the literary forms, the short story is the least intimidating and the most approachable.

Great literature is an important part of our human heritage. In the belief that this heritage belongs to everyone, *Lake Classic Short Stories* are adapted for today's readers. Lengthy sentences and paragraphs are shortened. Archaic words are replaced. Modern punctuation and spellings are used. Many of the longer stories are abridged. In all the stories, painstaking care has been taken to preserve the author's unique voice.

Lake Classic Short Stories have something for everyone. The hundreds of stories in the collection cover a broad terrain of themes, story types, and styles. Literary merit was a deciding factor in story selection. But no story was included unless it was as enjoyable as it was instructive. And special priority was given to stories that shine light on the human condition.

Each book in the *Lake Classic Short Stories* is devoted to the work of a single author. Little-known stories of merit are included with famous old favorites. Taken as a whole, the collected authors and stories make up a rich and diverse sampler of the story-teller's art.

Lake Classic Short Stories guarantee a great reading experience. Readers who look for common interests, concerns, and experiences are sure to find them. Readers who bring their own gifts of perception and appreciation to the stories will be doubly rewarded.

🌿 Honoré de Balzac 🌿
(1799–1850)

About the Author

Honoré de Balzac was born in Tours, France. When he was 15 his family moved to Paris.

After a few years as a lawyer's clerk, Balzac became interested in printing. But his love of romantic literature soon drew him to the writer's trade. At the age of 30, he began to work on *The Human Comedy*. This huge project would turn out to be one of the great literary monuments of all time.

As time went on, *The Human Comedy* grew into a huge collection of novels and stories. More than 2,000 characters people its pages. The plots describe in detail people of all social levels and occupations. As a whole, the work is a social history of Balzac's times.

For 20 years Balzac worked without stop on *The Human Comedy*. He wrote for 16 hours a day, sometimes without leaving his room for three days at a time. Usually he would have dinner at five, sleep until midnight, and then work all night and most of the next day. He died at age 50, worn out from overwork.

Balzac was a perfectionist. It is said that he rewrote his finished work time and time again. Printers charged him a fortune for making so many changes. But the pains he took resulted in greatness. The critic Taine paid him this high praise: "After Shakespeare, he is our great magazine of documents on human nature."

The short story "A Passion in the Desert" was written in 1831. It first appeared in a collection of stories called *Tales from the Military Life*.

The Mysterious Mansion

Do houses mirror the people who once lived in them? The grand old house in this story has gone to ruin. The story of what happened here will chill your bones.

FROM THE LOOK ON HER HUSBAND'S FACE, SHE KNEW
THERE WOULD BE TROUBLE.

The Mysterious Mansion

It stands about 100 yards from the town of Vendôme. The old gray house is completely set apart from any other houses in the neighborhood.

In front of this building, overlooking the Loire River, is a garden. Once, the garden walks were lined with boxes full of well-trimmed plants. Now, the boxes are broken and the plants are growing wild. The willow trees and the hedge that surrounds the garden are all overgrown. These trees hide more than half of the house. Weeds cover the grounds all the way from the house to the river.

The fruit trees in the garden have not been well tended. For the last 10 years, they have produced no fruit. Paths that used to be smooth are now mounded with moss. To tell the truth, there is no trace of the paths anymore.

The ruins of an old castle stand at the top of a nearby hill. This place once belonged to the Dukes of Vendôme. From the castle ruins, you can see the wildly overgrown garden below. As you look, it strikes you that this plot of land was once the delight of a country gentleman. No doubt he grew roses and tulips and all kinds of plants. You can guess that he was also a lover of fine fruit.

Under some old trees is a table that time has not quite destroyed. This part of the garden suggests the joys of a peaceful country life. Happy times were once enjoyed here. A sundial on one of the walls completes the sweet sadness of the scene. On this sundial is the Latin message, *ultimam cogita*—"Think of the end!"

The roof of the house is falling in. The shutters on the windows are closed and locked. Weeds have drawn green lines in the cracks on the stairs. The locks and bolts are rusty. Sun, moon, winter, summer, and snow have slowly eaten away at the wood.

The sad silence that rules over all is broken only by birds, cats, rats, and mice. These animals are free to run all over the place. Here they fight and eat and live out their lives. Over everything an invisible hand seems to have written the word *mystery*.

If you looked at this house from the roadside, you would see a large door. Since the door has been closed for the past 10 years, the children of the town have riddled it with holes. Through the holes broken by the boys, you can see the inner courtyard. The same disorder can be seen there. Weeds grow around all the paving stones. The walls are full of big cracks. All of the steps are broken, the wire of the bell is rusted, and the water spouts are cracked.

What fire from heaven has fallen here? What judge has ordered that salt should be thrown on this house? What terrible wrong has happened here? Has France been betrayed? These are the questions we ask ourselves.

But we get no answer from the crawling things that haunt the place. A giant mystery surrounds the empty house, and the key to unlock it seems to be lost. I know only that the mansion used to be called the Grande Bretêch in times gone by.

One day, my good landlady told me the story of the mysterious mansion. I prepared myself to listen.

"Sir," she said, "it all began with the Emperor. He ordered Spanish prisoners of war to be brought to Vendôme. The government told me to provide a room for a young Spaniard. He had been sent here on parole.

"The man was free to leave the house every day, but he could not leave the town. He was a Spanish grandee, and nothing less! His name ended in *os* and *dia*, something like Burgos de Férédia. I have his name on my books. I can find it for you if you like.

"Such a handsome young man he was! He was only a little over five feet tall, but he was well built. He had small hands that he took such good care of! You should have seen them! He had as many brushes for his hands as a woman has for her hair and clothes!

"The man had thick black hair and fiery eyes. His skin was beautiful. He wore the finest clothing I have ever seen on anyone. He didn't eat much, but his manners were so polite that you couldn't help but like him. I was very fond of him, even though he didn't open his lips four times in the day. It was impossible to have a conversation with him. If you spoke to him, he did not answer.

"He went to church every day. And where did he sit? Two steps from the chapel of Madame de Merret! No one suspected he was interested in her. He never took his eyes off his prayer book. In the evening, he would walk in the mountains. It was his only amusement, poor young man! It reminded him of his own country, no doubt. They say that Spain is all mountains!

"From the beginning of his time here, he stayed out late. At first, I was nervous when I found that he did not come home before midnight. But we got used to this. Soon he took the key of the door along with him. Then we stopped waiting up for him.

"One of our stable-men told us that he had seen the Spanish grandee one evening. The stable-man had taken the horses down to the water. He was looking out across the river when he saw the prisoner. The man was swimming far down the river like a live fish! Later I said something about it to him. He seemed annoyed that someone saw him in the water.

"At last, one day, or rather one morning, we did not find him in his room. He had not returned. After searching everywhere, I found a letter in the drawer of a table. With the letter were 50 pieces of Spanish gold called *doubloons*. They were worth about 5,000 francs. And in that drawer too were 10,000 francs' worth of diamonds in a small sealed box!

"The letter told us what to do in case he did not return. It said that the money and the diamonds were ours. He asked only that we pay the priest for some masses to thank God for his escape. My husband kept on searching for him.

"And now for the strangest part of the story. Later that day my husband brought back the Spaniard's clothes. He had found them under a big stone by the river near the castle. After reading the letter, my husband burned the clothes. We told everybody that the Spaniard had escaped.

"The police tried to find him, but they never could. Some people believed that the handsome young man had drowned himself. I, sir, don't think so. I think he had something to do with the story I heard about Madame de Merret.

"You see, my friend Rosalie was a servant of Madame de Merret. She told me that Madame had a crucifix made of ebony and silver. She thought so much of this crucifix that she had it buried with her. Now in the beginning of his stay here, Monsieur de Férédia had a crucifix made of ebony and silver. After he had been here for some time, I never again saw him with that crucifix.

"Now Rosalie never says much. That woman is like a wall! Even if she knows something, she won't talk. All I know is that Madame de Merret was buried with a crucifix of ebony and silver."

After telling me this story, my landlady left. I found myself thinking unsettled and gloomy thoughts. I was curious about the rest of the story, but it seemed like a mystery that I would never solve.

Suddenly I thought again of the old mansion. Its tall weeds, its barred windows, and its closed doors came to my mind. I wanted to find the knot of its dark story and untie it.

In my eyes Rosalie became the most interesting person in Vendôme. As I studied her, I could see that she had some secret worry. I could not tell whether it was the germ of sorrow or of hope. Yet her manners were rough and unpolished. Her silly smile was not that of a criminal. If you had seen her, you would have called her innocent. No, I thought, I will not leave Vendôme without learning the history of the Grande Bretêche. To do this, I had to strike up a friendship with Rosalie, if I could.

"Rosalie," said I, one evening.

"Sir?"

"You are not married?"

She looked surprised.

"Oh, I can find plenty of men," she said, laughing. "But I don't often want to be made miserable!"

"You are too good-looking to be short of lovers. But tell me, Rosalie—why did you start working in an inn so soon after Madame de Merret died? Did she leave you nothing to live on?"

"Oh, yes! But, sir, my job is the best in all Vendôme!"

The answer was one of those that judges and lawyers would call "evasive." It seemed to me that the girl Rosalie was like the square in the middle of a chessboard. She was at the heart of the truth. Somehow she was tied up in the very knot of it! Getting to know Rosalie better became my chief goal. It was as if the last chapter of a novel was centered in this girl.

One morning I spoke to her. "Tell me all you know about Madame de Merret," I said.

"Oh, no!" she replied in terror. "Do not ask that of me, Monsieur Horace."

Her pretty face fell. Her clear, bright color faded. And her eyes lost their innocent brightness.

"Well, then," she said at last. "If you *must* have it so—I will tell you about it. But promise to keep my secret!"

"Done! My dear girl, I will keep your secret with the honor of a thief. You know, of course, that is the most loyal in the world."

If I were to tell you everything Rosalie said, it would take a very large book. So I shall shorten her story.

Madame de Merret's room at the Bretêche was on the ground floor. She had a closet built into the wall there. It was about four feet deep. Three months before the terrible events I am about to describe, Madame de Merret became ill. Because of this, her husband moved to another room on the same floor. In the evenings, it was his habit to spend a few hours at his club. There he would read the newspapers and talk about politics with his friends.

Well, this one evening, he came home two hours later than usual. His wife thought he was already at home, in bed and asleep. But he had been talking and playing pool with his friends. Since his wife's illness, he usually spoke to Rosalie when he came in for the night. He would ask if his wife had already gone to bed. Then he would go on to his own room. This night, however, he took it in his head to say good night to his wife in person.

At dinner, he had noticed that she was dressed very nicely. On his way to the club, it came to him that his wife's health was much better. In fact, he thought, she was even more beautiful than before. As husbands sometimes can be, he was somewhat slow in making this discovery. So on this night, instead of talking to Rosalie, he went right to his wife's room. His steps echoed loudly in the high-ceilinged hallway.

The Count was just about to turn the handle of his wife's door when he thought he heard something. It sounded like the closing of her closet door. But when he entered the room, Madame de Merret was alone by the fireplace. The husband thought that it might be Rosalie who was in the closet. But for some reason, he felt suspicious anyway. He looked very closely at his wife. In her eyes he saw a wild and hunted look.

"You are very late," she said. Her voice was usually pure and sweet. Now it seemed changed to him.

Monsieur de Merret did not reply, for at that moment Rosalie entered. It hit him like a thunderbolt. He walked around the room, passing from one window to the other. He kept his arms folded across his chest.

"Have you heard bad news? Are you ill?" he asked his wife. Rosalie went on helping her get ready for bed.

He kept silent.

"You may leave me now," Madame de Merret then said to Rosalie. "I will put my hair in curl papers myself."

From the look on her husband's face, she knew there would be trouble. She wished to be alone with him. When Rosalie was gone, Monsieur de Merret stood in front of his wife. He said coldly to her, "Madame, there is someone in your closet!"

She looked calmly at her husband and simply said, "No, sir."

Monsieur de Merret did not believe her. Yet his wife had never looked more pure or saintly than at that moment. He rose to open the closet door. Madame de Merret took his hand and looked at him sadly. Then she said, "If you find no one there, remember this—all will be over between us!" The great dignity of his wife's quiet manner stopped him. Now Monsieur de Merret looked at her with great respect.

"All right, Josephine," he said. "I will not go in there. In either case, it would separate us forever. Hear me! I know how pure you are at heart. I know that your life is a holy one. You would not commit so great a sin to save your life."

At these words Madame de Merret turned a sad and tired gaze upon her husband.

"Here, take your crucifix," he said. "Swear to me before God that there is no one in the closet. I will believe you. I will never open that door."

Madame de Merret took the crucifix and said, "I swear."

"Louder," said her husband. "Say, *'I swear before God that there is no one in that closet.'*"

She repeated the sentence calmly.

"That will do," said Monsieur de Merret, coldly.

A moment of silence passed before he spoke again. "I never saw this pretty toy before," he said as he picked up the black and silver crucifix.

"I found it at Duvivier's," she said. "He said that he bought it from a Spanish monk. It was last year, when all the prisoners passed through Vendôme."

"Ah!" said Monsieur de Merret, as he laid down the crucifix. Then he rang for Rosalie. She had been listening at the door the whole time, so she did not keep him waiting. Then Monsieur led the servant to the bay window that opened on to the garden.

He whispered to her, "Listen, Rosalie! I know that Gorenflot wishes to marry you. Lack of money is the only thing standing in his way. You said that you would marry him if he found work as a master mason.

"Well! Go and get him. Tell him to come here with his trowel and tools. And tell him to be sure to come alone. His fortune will be more than you even wished for. But above all, leave this room without talking. Otherwise—" He frowned. Rosalie started off, but he called her back.

"Here, take my key," he said to her. Then, in a thundering voice, he cried, "Jean!" In answer, Monsieur de Merret's personal servant came immediately. Under his breath, the Count said to Jean, "Come and tell me when everyone is asleep. And be sure they are *asleep*, do you hear?"

Now the Count had been keeping his eye on his wife the whole time. After Jean ran off, he returned to her side. He began to tell her about his game of pool and his evening at the club. When Rosalie returned, she found Monsieur and Madame de Merret talking in a very friendly way.

Just recently, the ceilings of all the rooms on the ground floor had been repaired. Plaster of Paris was hard to get in Vendôme, so the Count had bought a great deal of it. He knew that he could always sell whatever was left over. The fact that he had so much of it gave him the idea for what he was about to do.

"Sir, Gorenflot has arrived," Rosalie whispered to him.

"Show him in," said the Count in a loud voice.

Madame de Merret turned rather pale when she saw the mason.

"Gorenflot," said her husband. "Go and get some bricks from the coach house. Bring enough bricks to wall up the door of this closet. Afterward, you will use my leftover plaster of Paris to coat the wall." Then he called Rosalie and the workman aside.

"Listen, Gorenflot," he said quietly. "You will sleep here tonight. But tomorrow you will have a passport to a foreign country. I will direct you to a certain town. Before you leave, I shall give you 6,000 francs for your trip. You will stay 10 years in that town. If you do not like it, you may go to another—as long as it is in the same country. When you get to Paris, you will wait there for me. In Paris, I will sign a contract. The contract will promise you 6,000 more francs on your return. But to claim the rest of the money, you must live up to the terms of our agreement. I am paying you to remain silent about what you will do tonight.

"As to you, Rosalie—I will give you 10,000 francs on the day of your marriage to Gorenflot. But, if you wish to marry, both of you must hold your tongues—or you will get no money."

"Rosalie," called Madame de Merret from across the room, "do my hair."

The husband walked calmly up and down. He watched the door, the mason, and his wife. He never showed that he doubted his wife's word. Madame de Merret waited until her husband was at the other end of the room. Then she said to Rosalie, "I will give you 1,000 francs a year, my child. Just tell Gorenflot to leave a space at the bottom." Then, out loud, she added, "Go and help him!"

All the time that Gorenflot was working, Monsieur and Madame de Merret were silent. This silence was deliberate on the part of the Count. His wife must have no chance to say anything with a double meaning. When the wall was about halfway up, Gorenflot saw that the Count's back was turned. Then he used his trowel to break one of the glass panes of the closet door. This act was a message to Madame de Merret. It told her that Rosalie had spoken to Gorenflot.

Behind the broken pane all three saw a man's face. It was a dark and gloomy face with black hair and eyes of flame. Before her husband turned, the poor woman had time to make a sign to the stranger. That sign said, *Hope!*

At 4 o'clock, toward dawn, the work was finished. The mason then left, and Monsieur de Merret went to bed in his wife's room.

When he got up in the morning, the Count said, "I must go to get Gorenflot's passport." He put on his hat and walked three steps toward the door. Then he changed his mind and came back. He took the crucifix.

His wife trembled with joy. "But he is going to Duvivier," she thought. As soon as the Count had left, Madame de Merret rang for Rosalie. When the servant arrived, Madame de Merret cried, "The trowel, the trowel! And let's be quick! I saw how Gorenflot did it. We shall have just enough time to make a hole and to mend it again."

In a moment, Rosalie brought the tools to her mistress. With all her strength, Madame de Merret started to knock out some of the bricks. She was getting ready to strike another strong blow when she felt that Monsieur de Merret was standing behind her. She fainted.

"Lay Madame on her bed," said the Count coldly. He had guessed what would happen when he left. She had fallen into the trap he had set for her. In fact, he had simply written to the mayor. And he had sent a servant for Duvivier. The jeweler arrived just as the room had been put in order.

"Ah, Duvivier!" the Count said in greeting. "Did you buy crucifixes from the Spaniards who passed through here?"

"No, sir."

"That will do, thank you," he said. He looked at his wife with the face of a tiger. "Jean," he went on, "from now on you will see that my meals are served in my wife's room. She is ill. I shall not leave her until she is better."

The cruel gentleman stayed with his wife for 20 days. In the beginning, a few weak sounds came from the walled closet. Josephine tried to beg his pity for the dying man. But the Count was very firm. Without allowing her to say a word, he kept repeating:

"You have sworn on the cross that no one is there."

The Thing at Ghent

A sick old woman has just moments left to live. Her relatives are amazed when she leaps up from her deathbed. What in the world is she trying to hide?

NONE OF THEM DARED TO LEAVE HER BEDSIDE. THEY
WERE AFRAID SHE MIGHT CHANGE HER WILL.

The Thing at Ghent

A strange thing took place at Ghent while I was staying there. A woman who had been a widow for 10 years lay dying. Three of her relatives stood around her bed, waiting for her last sigh. As her heirs, they were anxious to inherit her money. None of them dared to leave her bedside. They were afraid she would change her will at the last moment. Some of them thought she might leave all her money to a convent in the town.

The sick woman was silent. She seemed to be sleeping. Death was slow in coming. Can you imagine those three relatives seated in silence throughout the night?

An old nurse was with them. She looked at the sick woman and shook her head. The doctor also saw that the end was near. He made a sign to the relatives. That sign seemed to say, "I have no more visits to make here."

The silence in the room was broken only by howling winds. A snow storm was beating on the shutters. The youngest heir thought that the eyes of the dying woman might be dazzled by the light. So a shade had been fitted to the candle. Now the candlelight barely reached the pillow of the death bed. The sick woman's pale face stood out like a golden figure of Christ on a cross of tarnished silver.

The crackling fire gave off flickering rays of light. It seemed that the drama of the woman's life was ending at last. But then a log from the fire suddenly rolled onto the floor. It seemed to be a warning of some kind. At the sound of it, the sick woman quickly sat up. She opened her eyes. They were as clear as those of a cat.

Everyone in the room looked at her. They were astonished. Before anyone could stop her, the sick woman jumped out of the bed. She grabbed the tongs from the hearth and threw the log back into the fireplace.

The nurse, the doctor, and the three heirs rushed to help her. They put the dying woman back in bed. They laid her head on her pillow. In just a few minutes, she died. Yet, even after her death, her eye was fixed on a certain spot on the floor. It was the exact place where the burning log had rolled. Now the three heirs looked at each other with some suspicion.

Forgetting about their aunt, they began to inspect the mysterious floor. In low voices, the three heirs then made an agreement. They promised that none of them should leave the room. A servant was sent out to get a carpenter. The heirs' hearts beat wildly as they gathered around the flooring. They watched the carpenter strike the floor with his chisel.

At last the wood was cut through.

"My aunt made a sign," said the youngest.

"No, it was just the light that made it look that way," said the oldest. This heir kept one eye on the floor and the other on the dead body.

The heirs finally saw something beneath the flooring. A bulky object lay under the floor boards where the log had fallen. It was wrapped in a mass of plaster, like a work of art.

"Go on," said the oldest of the heirs.

The chisel of the carpenter then went to work again. A human head and some odds and ends of clothing were brought to light. The three heirs recognized their uncle, the Count. The whole town had thought that he had died on the island of Java. His loss had been bitterly mourned by his wife.

A Passion
in the Desert

Can love and fear be a
dangerous combination? In
this story an escaped soldier
gets lost in the Egyptian
desert. He struggles to
survive. But how can he
trust his strange, beautiful
companion?

THE BEAUTIFUL DESERT ANIMAL WAS PEACEFUL AND
FRIGHTENING AT THE SAME TIME.

A Passion in the Desert

"The whole show is dreadful!" she cried. We had just been watching the animal show of Mr. Martin. He was "working with his hyena," to speak in the style of the program.

"How does he think he can tame these animals enough to be so sure of their love for him?" she continued.

I felt I had to say something. "What seems to be a problem to you is really quite natural."

"Oh!" she cried in disbelief. Then she smiled at me.

"You think that animals have no passions?" I asked her. "It is quite the opposite. They have feelings just like you and me."

She looked at me as if she didn't believe me.

"Even so," I continued, "the first time I saw Mr. Martin, I felt the same as you do. I acted just as you did. But then I looked around. I found myself next to an old soldier whose right leg had been amputated. His lean face was very interesting. It was one of those faces on which the battles of Napoleon are written. And the old man had that honest, cheerful look that I always like to see.

"Without doubt he was one of those people who are surprised at nothing. He looked like the kind of man who could stand, laughing, in the middle of a battle. He looked like one of those men who doesn't waste time thinking too much.

Do you know the type? He would not be afraid to make friends with the devil himself.

"After we had both watched Mr. Martin's act, I remarked on the animal trainer's great courage. The old soldier smiled. He shook his head knowingly, and said, 'It's easy to understand.'

"'What do you mean?' I asked. 'Would you be kind enough to explain it to me?'

"We spoke for a few minutes and introduced ourselves. Then we went to eat at the first restaurant that caught our eye. For dessert, we ordered a bottle of champagne. That helped to brighten up the old soldier's memories. By the time he finished his story, I had to say that he was right. Just as he said, 'It was easy to understand.'"

I had just walked my friend to her door. Now she asked me to tell her the story. She made so many promises that I agreed to do so. The next day, I told her the story I am about to tell you. One might call it "The Frenchman in Egypt."

* * *

During the war in Upper Egypt, a French soldier fell into the hands of the Arabs. They carried him into the deserts beyond the falls of the Nile.

The Arabs wanted to get far away from the French army as quickly as possible. To do this they made forced marches, resting only at night. They camped around a well surrounded by palm trees. Under these trees, they had hidden a store of supplies. They had no idea that their prisoner would try to escape in the desert. So they simply tied his hands and left him alone. After eating a few dates and taking care of their horses, the Arabs went to sleep.

Soon the brave soldier saw that his enemies were not watching him. He used his teeth to steal a sword. Then he held the blade between his knees and cut the rope that was tied around his wrists.

Once his hands were free, the prisoner grabbed a rifle and a dagger. Then he took a sack of dried dates, oats, and some bullets. He tied a sword to his waist and leaped onto a horse. In a moment he was headed out. He was riding toward the French army as fast as he could.

The soldier was so eager to get back that he pushed the horse too hard. At last the poor animal stumbled and died. Now the Frenchman was left alone in the vast, empty desert.

For some time he walked in the sand. He called on all the courage of an escaped convict. But finally he had to stop, as the day had ended. He stared at the beauty of the night sky. Luckily he had come to a small hill with some palm trees at the top. Seen from afar, it was the greenness of the palms that had brought hope to his heart. Yet he felt he was not strong enough to go on.

He was so tired that he lay down on a

big rock. It was cut almost like a camp bed. There he fell asleep without even thinking about hiding. He had done the boldest deed of his life, yet his last thought was one of regret. He felt sorry for leaving the Arabs. Now that he was alone and without help, their wandering life seemed to smile on him.

The soldier was awakened by the sun. Its burning rays fell on the rock and made it very hot. He had been so stupid! Why had he made his bed in a place where the trees would cast no morning shadow? Now he looked at the trees and shuddered.

For something to do, he counted the palm trees. Then he looked around him, and he felt a wave of horrible despair. Before him stretched an ocean of sand without an end. The dark desert spread farther than he could see in any direction. It glittered like steel struck with a bright light.

It seemed to him that the desert might have been a sea of looking glass. Or it might have been many lakes melted together in a mirror. And the desert sky was lit in a strange way. It seemed that both heaven and earth were on fire.

The silence was awful, wild, and terrible. Now the entire universe seemed to close in upon him from every side. There was not a cloud in the sky, not a breath in the air. The horizon looked like it does at sea on a clear day. It was one line of light—as straight and unforgiving as the cut of a sword.

The soldier threw his arms around the trunk of a palm tree. He hugged it as if it were the body of a friend. In the thin shadow cast by the tall tree, he wept. He thought about the scene before him with deep sadness. Then he cried aloud, to measure the quiet. His voice was lost in the hollows of the hill. It sounded only faintly and made no echo. The only echo he heard was in his own heart. The soldier was 22 years old. He quietly loaded his rifle.

"There will be time enough for that," he said to himself. Then he placed his rifle on the ground. Perhaps it would be this weapon alone that could bring him peace.

Looking out at the lonely desert, the soldier dreamed of France. In his mind, he delighted to smell the gutters of Paris. He remembered the towns the army had passed. He thought of the faces of his fellow soldiers. The smallest details of his old life came back to him. He remembered even the stones on the streets of his beloved home town. He imagined that he could now see them under his feet.

Then suddenly he awoke from his dream. He knew that it had been a cruel mirage—and he was afraid of it. To shake himself up, he ran down the other side of the hill. There he found a cave. Inside it, he found the remains of an old rug. Someone else must have stayed here! A short distance away, he saw some palm trees full of dates. Slowly the will to live woke again in his heart. Hope returned in a rush. He resolved to live long enough to hear the sound of cannons again. At this time the armies of Napoleon were conquering Egypt.

This goal gave him new life. The palm tree seemed to bend with the weight of the ripe fruit. He shook some of it down. When he tasted the dates, he felt sure that someone had been tending the palms. The delicious, fresh taste of the dates proved it. His mind lifted at once from dark despair to an almost insane kind of joy.

Again the soldier went up to the top of the hill. There he spent the rest of the day cutting down a palm tree. As he worked, a vague memory made him think about the animals of the desert. He thought that they might come to drink at the spring. To protect himself from their visits, he placed a barrier between himself and the spring.

In spite of his hard work and his fear, he could not cut the palm into pieces. He was only able to cut it down. The sound of the tree falling could be heard far and wide. It seemed like a sign in the silence. Now the soldier shuddered. He felt that the sound was a voice warning of danger.

But he was like an heir who does not mourn long for a dead parent. Quickly he tore the leaves from the tree. He used them to mend his sleeping mat.

Then, tired out by his work and the terrible heat, he fell asleep under the red curtains of his wet cave.

In the middle of the night, his sleep was broken. He sat up when he heard a strange and terrible noise. But now the deep silence around him was filled by a strange breathing sound. He could tell that the breathing was not that of a human being.

His deep terror was made worse by the darkness, the silence, and his own imagination. His heart felt frozen within him. The soldier felt his hair stand on end. Straining his eyes as much as he could, he looked all around. Finally, through the shadows, he saw two faint yellow lights.

At first, he thought the lights were his own imagination. But slowly he was able to make out the objects around him. Now he could see a huge animal lying just two steps away. Was it a lion, a tiger, or a crocodile?

The soldier was not a well-educated man. He didn't know what kind of animal it was. This made him all the more frightened. His ignorance led him to imagine all terrors at once. Now he went through a cruel torture. Without daring to move, he noted every change in the animal's breathing.

An odor filled the cave. It was something like that of a fox, but deeper.

As the soldier thought about it, his terror reached its height. He could no longer doubt that a terrible companion was near. Now it came to him that the cave had belonged to this creature before he himself had found it.

After some time bright moonlight shone into the cave. It was then that the soldier could see the spotted coat of a panther—the lion of Egypt.

Curled up like a big dog, the panther slept. Its eyes opened for a moment and then closed again. Its face was turned toward the man. A thousand confused thoughts passed through the soldier's mind. First, he thought of killing it with a bullet from his gun. But he saw that there was not enough distance to take proper aim. His shot would certainly miss its mark.

But what if the animal were to wake? The thought made his arms and legs stiffen. He listened to his own heart beating in the silence. He cursed its loud thumping. What if his heartbeat disturbed the sleeping animal? He would not have enough time to escape!

Twice he placed his hand on his sword. Should he slice off the head of his enemy? But the difficulty of cutting through that stiff, short hair made him forget this daring plan. To miss would be to die for *certain*. He thought he'd do better in a fair fight. At last he made up his mind to wait for morning. But morning was coming fast. It did not leave him long to wait.

The soldier could now look at the panther easily. He saw that its nose and mouth were covered with blood.

"She's had a good dinner," he thought to himself. It didn't come to him that the animal might have feasted on human flesh. "She won't be hungry when she gets up."

The panther was a female. The fur on her belly and flanks was glistening white. Many small marks formed beautiful bracelets around her feet. Her tail was also white, ending in black rings. The upper part of her body was golden yellow. The animal was very graceful and as soft as velvet. The markings on her body set her apart from every other kind of cat.

The beautiful animal was peaceful and frightening at the same time. She snored as gracefully as a cat lying on a cushion. Her bloodstained paws were stretched out before her. Her face radiated straight, slender whiskers. They were as lovely as threads of silver.

If the panther had been in a cage, the soldier would have admired her grace. He would have enjoyed the beautiful coloring that gave her coat such a royal appearance. But just then, he was too troubled to feel anything but fear.

Even asleep, the presence of the panther was frightening. She produced a strange effect on him. It was the same effect the eyes of the serpent are said to have on the nightingale.

For a moment the courage of the soldier began to fail. He would have been less frightened if he had been facing a cannon. But then a bold thought brought daylight to his soul. This thought stopped the cold sweat that was beading up on his brow. Like many men who are facing death, he resolved to play his part with honor to the last.

"Just the day before yesterday, the Arabs could have killed me," he thought. So was he not already as good as dead? Now he decided to wait bravely—and with some stirrings of curiosity—for the panther to wake up.

When the sun appeared, the panther suddenly opened her eyes. She put out her paws with energy. It seemed that she wanted to stretch them to get rid of a cramp. At last she yawned, showing her teeth. Her pointed tongue looked as rough as a file.

"A regular little sweetheart," thought

the soldier, watching her roll around softly. She licked off the blood that stained her paws and mouth. She scratched her head with a smooth, beautiful movement.

"All right, go through your morning routine," the soldier said to himself. "When you're ready, we'll say good morning to each other."

Then he picked up the small, short dagger that he had taken from the Arabs. At that moment, the panther turned her head toward the man. She stared at him without moving.

The look in her eyes made him shudder, especially when she started to walk toward him. But the soldier looked at her with tenderness. He stared into her eyes as if he hoped to hypnotize her.

The soldier let the big animal come quite close to him. Then he passed his hand over her whole body. It was a moment both gentle and loving, as though he were caressing a loved one. He touched her from head to tail, scratching the spine that divided the panther's yellow back. The animal waved her tail slowly. Her eyes grew gentle. When the soldier petted her for the third time, she started to purr. This purr was nothing at all like the sound a housecat makes. Coming from such a powerful throat, it echoed through the cave like an organ in a church.

The man understood quite well the importance of his caresses. Quickly he gave her some more of them. When he felt sure that she would not attack him, he got up to go out of the cave. The panther allowed him to pass by. But when he had reached the top of the hill, he saw her springing along behind him. The big animal ran with the lightness of a sparrow hopping from twig to twig. She rubbed herself against his legs. She put up her back in the way that all cats do. Then she looked at her guest. The glare in her eyes had softened a little. Her cry made the sound that some people would compare to the grating of a saw.

"She really likes to be petted," said the soldier, smiling.

He was bold enough to play with her ears. Then he rubbed her belly and scratched her big head as hard as he could.

When he saw that she liked it, he tickled her skull with the point of his dagger. All the while he was watching for the right moment to kill her. But the hardness of her bones made him nervous. He wasn't sure he could cut through those heavy bones.

The queen of the desert was gracious to her new slave. She lifted her head, stretched out her neck, and showed her delight by her calm attitude. Suddenly the soldier knew that there was just one way to kill this savage princess with one blow. He must cut her throat.

The soldier raised his blade. But then the panther laid herself gracefully at his feet. She looked up at him with glances of innocence and good will. The poor soldier ate his dates, leaning against one of the palm trees. He kept looking out at the desert and back to the panther. What should he do?

The panther looked at the place where the date pits fell. Every time the soldier threw one down, her eyes showed a terrible mistrust.

She looked at the man in an almost loving way. When he finished his little meal, he stretched out his feet. She licked his boots with her powerful rough tongue. With great skill she brushed off all the dust that had gathered in the creases.

"Ah, but what happens when she's really hungry!" thought the soldier. He trembled at this thought. But then he began to study the panther. She was certainly a beautiful specimen of her kind. He judged that she was three feet high and four feet long, not counting her tail. The powerful tail, rounded like a club, was nearly three feet long itself. Her head, as large as that of a lion, had a strange look of refinement.

It was true that something of the cold cruelty of a tiger was in her face. But there was also something there like the face of a beautiful woman. Indeed, this lonely queen had something of the look of a drunken Nero. She had satisfied herself with blood—and now she wanted to play.

The soldier tried to walk up and down, and the panther let him do so. She seemed happy just to follow him with her eyes. In that she was less like a faithful dog than a big Angora cat. She watched every movement that her master made.

When he looked around, he saw the remains of his horse by the spring. The panther had dragged the body all that way! About two thirds of the poor horse had been eaten already. The sight of it made the soldier feel a little more comfortable.

The panther's meal explained why he had not seen her earlier. It also explained the respect she had had for him while he slept. He knew he had been lucky. Now he had the wild hope that he might be able to tame her. All day he tried to do this while remaining in her good graces.

As he walked back to her, he had the great joy of seeing her wag her tail. Then, without fear, he sat down by her side. They began to play together. He held her paws and face, pulled her ears, and stroked her warm flanks. She let him do whatever he liked. When he stroked the hair on her feet, she carefully drew in her claws.

Keeping his dagger in one hand, the man thought he would plunge it into her belly. But he was afraid. Perhaps she would strangle him in her last struggles.

Besides, he felt a growing respect in his heart for this creature that had done him no harm. How strange it was! Here in a boundless desert, he seemed to have found a friend.

Somehow the panther made him think of his first young sweetheart. He had nicknamed the girl "Mignonne," which means small and delicate, a little darling. The name was a joke between them because the girl was always so jealous. When she was angry she had sometimes threatened him with a small dagger. Now the love and fear he had for the panther suggested the same nickname.

Soon after he began to call the panther "Mignonne," she started answering to the name.

At the setting of the sun, Mignonne gave a deep, sad cry. "She's been well brought up," thought the soldier. "I see that she says her prayers!" But this joke only came to him when he saw how peaceful his companion was. "Come, my little darling. I'll let you go to bed first," he said to her. But he was thinking about the strength of his own legs. It was his plan to run away as soon as she was asleep. In some place far away he was hoping he could find another shelter for the night.

The soldier waited. When he heard the panther snoring, he walked in the direction of the Nile River. But hardly had he gone a mile when he heard the panther running after him. She was crying with the sawlike cry that was even more frightening than her growl.

"Ah!" he said. "She really likes me. Maybe she has never met a human being before. It is really quite flattering to have her first love."

Just then, the soldier stepped into one of those terrible desert quicksands. It is impossible to save oneself from one of these sinking pits. Feeling himself caught, he gave a shriek of terror. The panther grabbed him by the collar with her teeth. Then, springing strongly backward, she pulled him out of the whirling sand. It was like magic.

"Ah, Mignonne!" cried the soldier, petting her smooth back. "Now we're bound together for life and death!" Then he went back with her to the cave.

From that time on the desert seemed less lonely to him. Now there was a being to whom he could talk. Slowly she was made gentle by him. Even to himself he could not explain their strange sort of friendship. As much as the soldier wished to stay awake and on guard, he soon fell asleep.

When he woke up, he could not find Mignonne. He walked to the top of the hill. In the distance, he could see her springing toward him. When she arrived, he saw that her jaws were covered with blood. He patted her lovingly. With much purring she showed how happy she was to see him. Her eyes turned toward the soldier. They were even more gentle than the day before. Now he talked to her as he would talk to a tame animal.

"Ah! Mademoiselle, you are a nice girl, aren't you? Just look at that! So we like to be made much of, don't we? There, there, that's a darling!"

She allowed the soldier to play with her as a dog plays with its master. She let herself be rolled over, knocked about, and stroked. And sometimes she herself would put up her paw to him in a playful and friendly way.

Some days passed in this manner. This friendship allowed the soldier to appreciate the great beauty of the desert. Now he had plenty to eat and a living creature for company. Life became interesting again.

Solitude showed him all her secrets. It wrapped him in all her delights. In the rising and setting of the sun he discovered sights unknown to the world. He trembled in pleasure when he heard the hiss of a bird's wing overhead. Birds passed over so rarely!

He grew to appreciate the sight of clouds, changing and many-colored. For hours he would watch them melting into one another. In the night he studied how the moon looked on the ocean of sand. He saw the wind making waves that were swift of movement and rapid in their change. Sometimes the whirling sands looked like red, dry mists across the land. Every night he would welcome them with joy. For then he saw the glory of the stars and heard imaginary music in the skies.

Solitude also taught him to unroll the treasures of his dreams. He passed whole hours in remembering mere nothings and comparing his present life with his past.

At last he grew passionately fond of the panther. Some sort of affection, it seemed, was *necessary* to life.

For reasons that he could not quite understand, she respected the man's life. He began to fear the panther no longer, seeing her so well tamed.

The soldier spent most of his time sleeping. But it was the sleep of a spider in its web. Always he watched closely for his moment of escape. If anyone should pass the line marked by the horizon, he did not want to miss it.

He had used his shirt to make a flag. It was hung at the top of a palm tree whose leaves had been stripped. He used little sticks to keep the shirt fanned out, for the wind did not always blow. He wanted to be sure the passing traveler would not miss seeing the shirt.

Many were the long hours when he had lost hope. It was then that he amused himself with the panther. He had come to learn the different sounds of her voice. And he now knew all the expressions in her eyes.

Mignonne was not even angry when he took hold of her tail to count the rings. The rings glittered in the sun like jewelry. It pleased him to study the graceful lines of her body. But it was when she was playing that he felt most pleasure in looking at her. The amazing lightness of her movements was a constant surprise to him. He wondered at the way she jumped and climbed, washed herself, and arranged her fur. He even loved to watch her crouch down and prepare to spring. No matter what she was doing, however, she would always answer to the name "Mignonne."

One day, in a bright noontime sun, a huge bird flew through the air. The man left his panther to look at this new guest. But after waiting a moment, Mignonne growled deeply.

"My goodness! I do believe she's jealous!" the soldier thought. "It seems the soul of my old girlfriend has passed into her body."

The eagle disappeared into the air, as the soldier admired the curves of the panther. There was such youth and grace in her form! She was as beautiful as a woman! The blond fur of her back went well with the faint white markings on her legs.

The man and the panther stared at each other with a look full of meaning. She quivered when she felt her friend stroke her head. Her eyes flashed like lightning. Then she shut them tightly.

"She has a soul," he said, looking at her.

*   *   *

"Well," my friend said, "thank you for telling me your story. But what finally happened? How does the story of these two friends end?"

"Ah, well!" I said. "You see, it had to end as all great passions do. At last there was a misunderstanding. For some reason one suspects the other of treason. They don't talk about it because of pride.

Instead they quarrel and finally part. Just because they are both too stubborn to talk!"

"Yet sometimes," said my friend, "a single word or a look is enough. But, anyhow, go on with your story."

"It's terribly difficult, but you will understand. This is what the old soldier told me over his champagne.

"He said—'I don't know if I hurt her, but she turned around as if she were angry. With her sharp teeth, she caught hold of my leg. Her bite was gentle, as I remember it. But I was afraid she would hurt me. It was then that I plunged my dagger into her throat. She rolled over, giving a cry that froze my heart.

"'As she lay there dying, I saw that she was still looking at me without anger. I would have given all my world to have brought her to life again. It was as if I had murdered a real person. The soldiers who came to rescue me later found me in tears.'

"'Well, sir,' he said, after a moment of silence, 'since then I've been in many wars. I've traveled all around the world. But never have I seen anything like the desert. Ah, yes, it is very beautiful!'

"'But what did you *feel* there?' I asked him.

"'Oh, that can't be described, young man. Besides, I am not always regretting my time with my palm trees and my panther. I would be very sad all the time if I did. In the desert, you see, there is everything and nothing.'

"'Yes, but explain—'

"'Well,' he said, with an impatient gesture, 'it is God without mankind.'"

Thinking About
the Stories

The Mysterious Mansion

1. The plot is the series of events that takes place in a story. Usually, story events are linked in some way. Can you name an event in this story that was the cause of a later event?

2. What is the title of this story? Can you think of another good title?

3. Good writing always has an effect on the reader. How did you feel when you finished reading this story? Were you surprised, horrified, amused, sad, touched, or inspired? What elements in the story made you feel that way?

The Thing at Ghent

1. All stories fit into one or more categories. Is this story serious or funny? Would you call it an adventure, a love story, or a mystery? Is it a character study? Or is it simply a picture the author has painted of a certain time and place? Explain your thinking.

2. What period of time is covered in this story—an hour, a week, several years? What role, if any, does time play in the story?

3. Interesting story plots often have unexpected twists and turns. What surprises did you find in this story?

A Passion in the Desert

1. Does the main character in this story have an internal conflict? Does a terrible decision have to be made? Explain the character's choices.

2. Where does this story take place? Is there anything unusual about it? What effect does the place have on the characters?

3. All the events in a story are arranged in a certain order, or sequence. Tell about one event from the beginning of this story, one from the middle, and one from the end. How are these events related?

Thinking About

the Book

1. Choose your favorite illustration in this book. Use this picture as a springboard to write a new story. Give the characters different names. Begin your story with something they are saying or thinking.

2. Compare the stories in this book. Which was the most interesting? Why? In what ways were they alike? In what ways different?

3. Good writers usually write about what they know best. If you wrote a story, what kind of characters would you create? What would be the setting?